I0477895

Financial Foundations: A Beginner's Guide to Personal Finance

Chapter 1: Introduction to Personal Finance

What is Personal Finance?

Personal finance is the management of an individual's or a family's financial activities and decisions, including budgeting, saving, investing, and planning for the future. It encompasses all the financial decisions and activities of an individual or household, which include earning, spending, saving, investing, and protecting financial resources.

Understanding personal finance is crucial because it empowers you to make informed decisions about your money. It helps you create a roadmap for your financial future, ensuring you can meet both your short-term and long-term goals.

Key Components of Personal Finance

1. **Income**: The money you earn from various sources such as your job, business, investments, or other activities. Understanding your income is the first step in managing your finances effectively.
2. **Expenses**: These are the costs incurred for goods and services, including necessities like housing, food, and transportation, as well as discretionary spending like entertainment and dining out. Controlling your expenses is essential for maintaining financial health.
3. **Saving**: The portion of your income that you set aside for future needs or emergencies. Saving is critical for financial stability and achieving your financial goals.
4. **Investing**: Using your savings to purchase assets with the potential to generate returns over time. Investing is a key strategy for building wealth and securing your financial future.
5. **Protecting**: Measures taken to safeguard your financial resources, such as insurance and emergency funds. Protecting your finances ensures that unexpected events don't derail your financial plans.

Setting Financial Goals

Setting financial goals is the foundation of personal finance. Goals give you direction and a sense of purpose in managing your money. They can be short-term, medium-term, or long-term.

- **Short-term goals**: These are goals you plan to achieve within a year, such as saving for a vacation or paying off a small debt.
- **Medium-term goals**: These goals typically take one to five years to achieve, such as buying a car or saving for a wedding.
- **Long-term goals**: These are goals that take more than five years to accomplish, such as saving for retirement or buying a home.

To effectively set and achieve your financial goals, it's helpful to use the SMART criteria:

- **Specific**: Clearly define what you want to achieve.
- **Measurable**: Ensure you can track your progress.
- **Achievable**: Set realistic goals that are attainable.
- **Relevant**: Align your goals with your values and long-term objectives.
- **Time-bound**: Set a deadline for achieving your goals.

For example, instead of saying "I want to save money," a SMART goal would be "I want to save $5,000 for an emergency fund within the next 12 months."

The Financial Planning Process

Creating a financial plan involves several key steps:

1. **Assess Your Current Financial Situation**: Review your income, expenses, savings, debts, and investments. Understanding where you stand financially is the first step in creating a plan.
2. **Set Financial Goals**: Based on your assessment, set realistic and achievable short-term, medium-term, and long-term goals.
3. **Develop a Plan**: Outline the steps needed to achieve your goals. This might include creating a budget, setting up automatic savings, or developing an investment strategy.
4. **Implement Your Plan**: Put your plan into action. This involves following your budget, saving regularly, and making informed investment decisions.
5. **Monitor and Review Your Plan**: Regularly review your financial plan to ensure you're on track to meet your goals. Adjust your plan as needed based on changes in your financial situation or goals.

Conclusion

Personal finance is a journey that begins with understanding your financial situation and setting clear, achievable goals. By mastering the basics of income, expenses, saving, investing, and protecting your finances, you can create a solid foundation for your financial future. In the following chapters, we'll delve deeper into each of these components, providing you with the knowledge and tools needed to take control of your financial destiny.

Chapter 2: Budgeting Basics

Understanding Income and Expenses

Creating a successful budget begins with understanding your income and expenses. These are the fundamental elements of your financial picture.

- **Types of Income**:
    - **Earned Income**: Wages or salary from your job.

- **Passive Income**: Money earned with minimal effort, such as rental income or dividends.
- **Portfolio Income**: Earnings from investments, including stocks, bonds, and other securities.
- **Types of Expenses**:
  - **Fixed Expenses**: Regular, unchanging costs such as rent/mortgage payments, car payments, and insurance premiums.
  - **Variable Expenses**: Costs that fluctuate month-to-month, such as groceries, utilities, entertainment, and dining out.
  - **Discretionary Expenses**: Non-essential spending, such as vacations, hobbies, and luxury items.

Creating a Budget

A budget is a plan that outlines your income and expenses, helping you manage your money effectively. Here's how to set one up:

1. **Calculate Your Income**:
   - Include all sources of income: salary, bonuses, rental income, etc.
   - Use your net income (take-home pay) after taxes and deductions.
2. **List Your Expenses**:
   - Track all your expenses for a month to understand where your money is going.
   - Categorize expenses into fixed, variable, and discretionary.
3. **Set Your Goals**:
   - Determine what you want to achieve with your budget. This could include saving for an emergency fund, paying off debt, or saving for a vacation.
4. **Allocate Your Income**:
   - Distribute your income across different categories: essentials (housing, utilities, groceries), savings, debt repayment, and discretionary spending.
5. **Use a Budgeting Method**:
   - **50/30/20 Rule**: Allocate 50% of your income to needs, 30% to wants, and 20% to savings and debt repayment.
   - **Zero-Based Budget**: Every dollar is assigned a purpose until your income minus expenses equals zero.
   - **Envelope System**: Use cash envelopes for different spending categories to limit overspending.

Tracking and Adjusting Your Budget

Once you have created your budget, the next step is to track your spending and make adjustments as needed.

- **Tracking Tools and Apps**:
  - **Manual Tracking**: Use a spreadsheet or notebook to record your expenses.
  - **Budgeting Apps**: Popular apps like Mint, YNAB (You Need A Budget), and EveryDollar can simplify the process by automatically categorizing transactions and providing real-time updates.
- **Reviewing Your Budget**:
  - **Weekly Reviews**: Check your spending weekly to ensure you're staying on track.
  - **Monthly Reviews**: At the end of each month, compare your actual spending to your budget. Identify any discrepancies and adjust your budget for the following month.
- **Adjusting Your Budget**:
  - **Unexpected Expenses**: Adjust your budget to accommodate unexpected costs, such as car repairs or medical bills.
  - **Changes in Income**: If your income increases or decreases, revise your budget accordingly.
  - **Achieving Goals**: Once you reach a financial goal, reallocate funds to new goals or adjust spending as needed.

Tips for Successful Budgeting
- **Be Realistic**: Set attainable goals and be honest about your spending habits.
- **Prioritize Savings**: Treat savings as a fixed expense and automate it where possible.
- **Limit Discretionary Spending**: Identify areas where you can cut back to save more money.
- **Stay Flexible**: Life changes, and so should your budget. Be prepared to adjust as needed.
- **Involve Your Family**: If you share finances with a partner or family, make budgeting a joint effort to ensure everyone is on the same page.

Conclusion

Budgeting is a powerful tool that helps you take control of your finances. By understanding your income and expenses, setting clear goals, and tracking your progress, you can create a budget that works for you. Remember, a budget is not set in stone—it's a dynamic plan that should evolve with your financial situation. In the next chapter, we'll explore saving money and building an emergency fund, essential steps in achieving financial security.

Chapter 3: Saving Money

The Importance of Saving

Saving money is a cornerstone of financial health. It provides a safety net for emergencies, helps you achieve financial goals, and ensures a more secure future.

1. **Emergency Fund**: This is your financial buffer against unexpected expenses such as medical emergencies, car repairs, or job loss. Experts recommend having three to six months' worth of living expenses saved in an easily accessible account.
2. **Saving for Goals**: Whether it's buying a home, going on a vacation, or funding your education, saving helps you turn your financial dreams into reality.
3. **Financial Stability**: Regular saving habits lead to financial stability and peace of mind, reducing stress and increasing your ability to handle life's uncertainties.

Types of Savings Accounts

Understanding the different types of savings accounts can help you choose the best option for your needs.

1. **Traditional Savings Accounts**:
   - **Pros**: Easy to open, low minimum balance requirements, insured by the FDIC.
   - **Cons**: Low interest rates, limited to six withdrawals per month by federal regulation.
2. **High-Yield Savings Accounts**:
   - **Pros**: Higher interest rates compared to traditional savings accounts, also FDIC insured.
   - **Cons**: May have higher minimum balance requirements, same withdrawal limitations.
3. **Money Market Accounts**:
   - **Pros**: Higher interest rates, check-writing and debit card privileges.
   - **Cons**: Higher minimum balance requirements, possible fees, limited transactions.
4. **Certificates of Deposit (CDs)**:
   - **Pros**: Higher fixed interest rates for a set term, insured by the FDIC.
   - **Cons**: Funds are locked for a specific period (3 months to 5 years), penalties for early withdrawal.
5. **Specialty Savings Accounts**:
   - **Pros**: Tailored for specific goals like education (529

Plans) or health (HSAs).
- **Cons**: May have specific rules and limitations on how funds can be used.

Strategies for Saving

Implementing effective saving strategies can help you build your savings more efficiently.

1. **Automate Your Savings**:
   - **Direct Deposit**: Set up automatic transfers from your checking account to your savings account.
   - **Employer Contributions**: Utilize direct deposit to funnel a portion of your paycheck into a savings account.
2. **Pay Yourself First**:
   - Treat your savings like a non-negotiable bill. Allocate a portion of your income to savings before spending on anything else.
3. **Cut Unnecessary Expenses**:
   - Review your budget and identify areas where you can reduce spending. Redirect these savings to your savings account.
4. **Use Windfalls Wisely**:
   - Allocate bonuses, tax refunds, or monetary gifts to your savings rather than spending them.
5. **Set Specific Goals**:
   - Define what you're saving for and how much you need. This clarity can motivate you to stay disciplined.
6. **Track Your Progress**:
   - Regularly monitor your savings to see how close you are to reaching your goals. Adjust your savings rate as needed.

Tips to Increase Your Savings Rate

1. **Negotiate Bills**:
   - Contact service providers to negotiate lower rates for internet, phone, and insurance.
2. **Refinance Loans**:
   - Look into refinancing options for mortgages, car loans, or student loans to reduce interest rates and monthly payments.
3. **Buy in Bulk**:
   - Purchase non-perishable items in bulk to save money over time.
4. **Cook at Home**:
   - Reduce dining out and prepare meals at home to save money and eat healthier.

5. **Limit Subscriptions**:
   - Cancel unused subscriptions or switch to cheaper alternatives.

Conclusion

Saving money is an essential component of personal finance that provides security and enables you to achieve your financial goals. By understanding different savings options and implementing effective strategies, you can build a robust financial cushion. In the next chapter, we will delve into understanding and managing debt, another critical aspect of financial health.

Chapter 4: Understanding Debt

Types of Debt

Debt can be a useful financial tool when managed properly, but it can also become a burden if not handled with care. Understanding the different types of debt is crucial for effective management.

1. **Good Debt vs Bad Debt**:
   - **Good Debt**: Debt that can potentially increase your net worth or enhance your life in a meaningful way. Examples include student loans (for education) and mortgages (for home ownership).
   - **Bad Debt**: Debt incurred for items that don't generate income or appreciate in value. Examples include credit card debt for discretionary purchases and payday loans.
2. **Common Types of Debt**:
   - **Credit Card Debt**: Revolving debt with high-interest rates, used for everyday purchases.
   - **Student Loans**: Loans taken to pay for education, usually with lower interest rates and flexible repayment terms.
   - **Mortgages**: Loans used to purchase real estate, typically with lower interest rates and long repayment periods.
   - **Auto Loans**: Loans used to purchase vehicles, usually with moderate interest rates and shorter terms.
   - **Personal Loans**: Unsecured loans that can be used for various purposes, often with higher interest rates.

Managing Debt

Effective debt management involves understanding your debt, creating a plan to repay it, and making informed decisions to avoid accumulating unnecessary debt.

1. **Assess Your Debt Situation**:

- **List All Debts**: Include the balance, interest rate, and minimum monthly payment for each debt.
- **Calculate Your Debt-to-Income Ratio**: This ratio helps you understand how much of your income goes toward debt repayment. A ratio above 40% can be a sign of financial stress.

2. **Debt Repayment Strategies**:
   - **Debt Snowball Method**: Focus on paying off the smallest debts first while making minimum payments on larger debts. This method provides quick wins and boosts motivation.
   - **Debt Avalanche Method**: Focus on paying off the debts with the highest interest rates first while making minimum payments on other debts. This method saves money on interest in the long run.
   - **Debt Consolidation**: Combine multiple debts into a single loan with a lower interest rate. This can simplify payments and reduce interest costs.
   - **Refinancing**: Refinance high-interest loans (like mortgages or auto loans) to lower interest rates, reducing monthly payments and total interest paid over the life of the loan.

Credit Scores and Reports

Your credit score and credit report are crucial components of your financial health, affecting your ability to borrow money, rent an apartment, or even get a job.

1. **Understanding Credit Scores**:
   - **FICO Score**: The most commonly used credit score, ranging from 300 to 850. A higher score indicates better creditworthiness.
   - **Factors Affecting Your Credit Score**:
     - **Payment History**: On-time payments boost your score, while late or missed payments harm it.
     - **Credit Utilization**: The ratio of your current credit card balances to your credit limits. Lower utilization rates are better.
     - **Length of Credit History**: A longer credit history generally improves your score.
     - **Types of Credit**: A mix of credit types (credit cards, mortgages, auto loans) can positively impact your score.
     - **Recent Credit Inquiries**: Multiple recent

inquiries can lower your score.
2. **How to Improve Your Credit Score**:
    - **Pay Bills on Time**: Consistently making on-time payments is the most important factor in improving your credit score.
    - **Reduce Credit Card Balances**: Aim to keep your credit utilization below 30%.
    - **Avoid Opening New Accounts Frequently**: Too many new accounts can lower your average account age and lead to multiple inquiries.
    - **Check Your Credit Report**: Regularly review your credit report for errors and dispute any inaccuracies.
3. **Credit Reports**:
    - **Obtaining Your Credit Report**: You are entitled to a free credit report from each of the three major credit bureaus (Equifax, Experian, and TransUnion) once a year through AnnualCreditReport.com.
    - **Reviewing Your Credit Report**: Check for accuracy in your personal information, account details, and payment history. Dispute any errors promptly.

Conclusion

Understanding and managing debt is a critical aspect of maintaining financial health. By recognizing the types of debt, implementing effective repayment strategies, and keeping a close eye on your credit score and report, you can take control of your financial future. In the next chapter, we'll explore the basics of investing, a key step in building wealth and achieving long-term financial goals.

Chapter 5: Basics of Investing

Why Invest?

Investing is a crucial component of financial planning. It allows you to grow your wealth over time and achieve your long-term financial goals. Here are some key reasons why investing is important:
1. **The Power of Compound Interest**:
    - **Definition**: Compound interest is the interest on a loan or deposit calculated based on both the initial principal and the accumulated interest from previous periods.

- **Example**: If you invest $1,000 at an annual interest rate of 5%, you'll have $1,050 after one year. The next year, you'll earn interest on $1,050, not just the original $1,000. Over time, this compounding effect can significantly increase your investment.
2. **Inflation and Purchasing Power**:
   - **Definition**: Inflation is the rate at which the general level of prices for goods and services rises, eroding purchasing power.
   - **Impact**: If your money isn't growing at a rate that outpaces inflation, its purchasing power decreases over time. Investing helps your money grow and keeps pace with or exceeds inflation.
3. **Building Wealth**:
   - Investing is one of the most effective ways to build wealth. It provides the opportunity to earn higher returns compared to traditional savings accounts.

Types of Investments

There are various investment options available, each with its own risk and return characteristics. Here's an overview of some common types:
1. **Stocks**:
   - **Definition**: Stocks represent ownership in a company. When you buy a stock, you become a shareholder and own a piece of that company.
   - **Returns**: Potential for high returns through capital appreciation and dividends.
   - **Risks**: Prices can be volatile and are influenced by market conditions, company performance, and economic factors.
2. **Bonds**:
   - **Definition**: Bonds are debt securities issued by governments or corporations. When you buy a bond, you're lending money to the issuer in exchange for periodic interest payments and the return of the bond's face value at maturity.
   - **Returns**: Typically lower than stocks, but more stable. Interest payments provide regular income.
   - **Risks**: Interest rate risk, credit risk, and inflation risk.
3. **Mutual Funds**:
   - **Definition**: Mutual funds pool money from multiple investors to buy a diversified portfolio of stocks, bonds, or other securities managed by a professional fund manager.
   - **Returns**: Varies based on the fund's performance and the

underlying assets.
- **Risks**: Depends on the fund's investment strategy and the assets it holds. Market risk and management risk are key considerations.

4. **Exchange-Traded Funds (ETFs)**:
   - **Definition**: ETFs are similar to mutual funds but trade on stock exchanges like individual stocks. They offer a diversified portfolio of assets.
   - **Returns**: Varies based on the ETF's performance and the underlying assets.
   - **Risks**: Market risk, tracking error, and liquidity risk.

5. **Real Estate**:
   - **Definition**: Investing in property, either directly through ownership or indirectly through Real Estate Investment Trusts (REITs).
   - **Returns**: Potential for rental income and capital appreciation.
   - **Risks**: Market risk, property management issues, and liquidity risk.

6. **Other Alternative Investments**:
   - **Examples**: Commodities, hedge funds, private equity, and cryptocurrencies.
   - **Returns**: Can be high but vary widely.
   - **Risks**: Often higher risk and less liquidity compared to traditional investments.

Risk and Return

Understanding the relationship between risk and return is fundamental to investing.

1. **Risk Tolerance**:
   - **Definition**: Your risk tolerance is your ability and willingness to endure market fluctuations and potential loss of capital.
   - **Assessment**: Factors influencing risk tolerance include your financial goals, investment timeline, and emotional comfort with risk.

2. **Diversification**:
   - **Definition**: Diversification involves spreading your investments across different asset classes to reduce risk.
   - **Benefits**: Reduces the impact of poor performance in any single investment, leading to more stable returns.

3. **Balancing Risk and Return**:
   - **Asset Allocation**: The process of dividing your investment

portfolio among different asset categories (e.g., stocks, bonds, real estate) based on your risk tolerance and investment goals.

- **Rebalancing**: Periodically adjusting your asset allocation to maintain your desired risk level as market conditions change.

Getting Started with Investing

Here are some steps to help you begin your investing journey:

1. **Set Clear Goals**:
   - Define your investment objectives, such as retirement, buying a home, or funding education. Having clear goals helps determine your investment strategy.

2. **Educate Yourself**:
   - Learn about different investment options, risk management, and market dynamics. Resources include books, online courses, and financial news.

3. **Start Small**:
   - Begin with a modest amount of money and gradually increase your investments as you gain confidence and experience.

4. **Choose the Right Accounts**:
   - Consider tax-advantaged accounts like IRAs and 401(k)s for retirement savings. Regular brokerage accounts are suitable for other investment goals.

5. **Seek Professional Advice**:
   - If you're unsure where to start, consider consulting with a financial advisor. They can help you create a personalized investment plan.

6. **Stay Disciplined**:
   - Investing is a long-term commitment. Avoid reacting to short-term market fluctuations and stay focused on your goals.

Conclusion

Investing is a powerful tool for building wealth and achieving your financial goals. By understanding the basics of different investment options, assessing your risk tolerance, and starting with a clear plan, you can make informed decisions that will help you grow your wealth over time. In the next chapter, we will explore the stock market in more detail, providing you with the knowledge to navigate this important investment arena effectively.

Chapter 6: Navigating the Stock Market

Understanding the Stock Market
The stock market is a dynamic platform where investors buy and sell shares of publicly traded companies. It plays a crucial role in the economy, enabling companies to raise capital and investors to potentially earn returns.

1. **What is a Stock?**
   - **Definition**: A stock represents ownership in a company. When you buy a share of stock, you own a small part of that company and have a claim on part of its assets and earnings.
   - **Types of Stocks**:
     - **Common Stock**: Offers voting rights and potential dividends. Common stockholders are last to be paid in the event of liquidation.
     - **Preferred Stock**: Typically does not offer voting rights but provides a fixed dividend. Preferred stockholders are paid before common stockholders in liquidation.
2. **How the Stock Market Works**:
   - **Exchanges**: Stocks are traded on exchanges, such as the New York Stock Exchange (NYSE) and the Nasdaq. These platforms facilitate the buying and selling of stocks.
   - **Market Participants**: Include individual investors, institutional investors (like mutual funds and pension funds), market makers, and brokers.
   - **Market Hours**: Most stock exchanges operate during standard business hours, but some offer after-hours trading.

Key Concepts in Stock Investing
1. **Stock Prices**:
   - **Determination**: Stock prices are determined by supply and demand. Factors influencing prices include company performance, economic indicators, market sentiment, and geopolitical events.
   - **Volatility**: Stocks can be volatile, meaning their prices can fluctuate significantly in short periods. Understanding and managing this volatility is crucial for investors.
2. **Dividends**:
   - **Definition**: A portion of a company's earnings distributed

to shareholders. Not all companies pay dividends.
- **Yield**: Dividend yield is calculated as the annual dividend payment divided by the stock's current price. It provides insight into the income generated by the investment.

3. **Market Capitalization**:
   - **Definition**: The total market value of a company's outstanding shares. Calculated as stock price multiplied by the number of outstanding shares.
   - **Categories**:
     - **Large-Cap**: Companies with a market cap over $10 billion.
     - **Mid-Cap**: Companies with a market cap between $2 billion and $10 billion.
     - **Small-Cap**: Companies with a market cap below $2 billion.

4. **Price-to-Earnings (P/E) Ratio**:
   - **Definition**: A valuation metric calculated by dividing the stock price by the company's earnings per share (EPS). It indicates how much investors are willing to pay for a dollar of earnings.
   - **Interpretation**: A high P/E ratio may indicate that a stock is overvalued, while a low P/E ratio may suggest it's undervalued.

How to Invest in Stocks

1. **Choose an Investment Strategy**:
   - **Growth Investing**: Focuses on companies expected to grow at an above-average rate compared to other companies. Growth stocks often reinvest earnings into the business rather than paying dividends.
   - **Value Investing**: Seeks out undervalued stocks with strong fundamentals. Value investors look for stocks trading below their intrinsic value.
   - **Income Investing**: Focuses on stocks that provide regular income through dividends. Suitable for investors seeking steady cash flow.

2. **Opening a Brokerage Account**:
   - **Types of Brokers**:
     - **Full-Service Brokers**: Offer personalized advice and manage investments, typically for higher fees.
     - **Discount Brokers**: Provide fewer services but lower fees, suitable for self-directed investors.
   - **Account Types**:

- **Individual Brokerage Account**: A standard account for buying and selling stocks.
- **Retirement Accounts**: Such as IRAs, offering tax advantages for long-term savings.

3. **Research and Analysis**:
   - **Fundamental Analysis**: Evaluates a company's financial health and performance by analyzing financial statements, management, industry conditions, and other factors.
   - **Technical Analysis**: Studies historical price and volume data to predict future price movements. Uses charts and indicators like moving averages and relative strength index (RSI).

4. **Placing Trades**:
   - **Types of Orders**:
     - **Market Order**: Buys or sells immediately at the current market price.
     - **Limit Order**: Buys or sells at a specified price or better.
     - **Stop Order**: Executes a trade when the stock reaches a certain price.
   - **Timing**: Consider market conditions and news events before placing trades.

Risk Management

1. **Diversification**:
   - **Definition**: Spreading investments across various assets to reduce risk. A diversified portfolio may include stocks from different sectors, bonds, real estate, and other assets.
   - **Benefits**: Reduces the impact of poor performance in any single investment.

2. **Risk Tolerance**:
   - Assess your comfort level with risk based on your financial situation, investment goals, and timeline. Adjust your portfolio accordingly to match your risk tolerance.

3. **Regular Monitoring and Rebalancing**:
   - **Monitoring**: Regularly review your investments to ensure they align with your goals.
   - **Rebalancing**: Adjust your portfolio periodically to maintain your desired asset allocation. This might involve selling assets that have increased in value and buying those that have decreased.

Conclusion

Navigating the stock market requires a solid understanding of how it operates, the key concepts involved, and effective investment strategies. By choosing the right approach, conducting thorough research, and managing risk appropriately, you can harness the potential of the stock market to grow your wealth over time. In the next chapter, we will explore bonds and other fixed-income investments, providing a comprehensive guide to these more stable investment options.

Chapter 7: Bonds and Fixed-Income Investments

Understanding Bonds

Bonds are a key component of many investment portfolios, providing a stable source of income and reducing overall portfolio risk. Here's an overview of how bonds work:

1. **What is a Bond?**
   - **Definition**: A bond is a loan made by an investor to a borrower (typically a corporation or government). In return, the borrower promises to pay periodic interest and repay the principal at maturity.
   - **Components**:
     - **Face Value (Par Value)**: The amount the bond will be worth at maturity; also the amount on which interest payments are calculated.
     - **Coupon Rate**: The interest rate that the bond issuer will pay to the bondholder.
     - **Maturity Date**: The date when the bond will mature, and the issuer will repay the bondholder the face value of the bond.
     - **Issuer**: The entity that issues the bond, such as a corporation, municipality, or government.
2. **Types of Bonds**:
   - **Government Bonds**: Issued by national governments and considered low-risk.
     - **Treasury Bonds (T-Bonds)**: Long-term government bonds with maturities of 10 years or more.
     - **Treasury Notes (T-Notes)**: Medium-term government bonds with maturities of 2 to 10 years.
     - **Treasury Bills (T-Bills)**: Short-term government bonds with maturities of one year or less.
   - **Municipal Bonds**: Issued by state and local governments. Often tax-exempt.
   - **Corporate Bonds**: Issued by corporations to raise capital.

These can range from high-quality (investment grade) to high-yield (junk bonds).

- **Agency Bonds**: Issued by government-affiliated organizations.
- **International Bonds**: Issued by foreign governments or companies. These carry additional risks such as currency risk.

How Bonds Generate Returns

1. **Interest Payments (Coupon Payments)**:
   - Bonds pay periodic interest, typically semi-annually, based on the coupon rate. This provides a predictable income stream.
2. **Capital Gains**:
   - If a bond is sold before maturity for more than its purchase price, the investor earns a capital gain. Conversely, selling for less than the purchase price results in a capital loss.

Bond Pricing and Yield

1. **Bond Prices**:
   - **Market Price**: The price at which a bond is currently trading in the market. Bond prices fluctuate based on interest rates, the issuer's creditworthiness, and market conditions.
   - **Premium and Discount**: If a bond's market price is above its face value, it's trading at a premium. If below, it's trading at a discount.
2. **Yield**:
   - **Current Yield**: The annual interest payment divided by the bond's current market price.
   - **Yield to Maturity (YTM)**: The total return anticipated if the bond is held until it matures, accounting for interest payments and any capital gain or loss.
   - **Yield to Call (YTC)**: The yield calculated if the bond is callable and is called before its maturity date.

Risks of Bond Investing

1. **Interest Rate Risk**:
   - Bond prices are inversely related to interest rates. When interest rates rise, bond prices fall, and vice versa. Longer-term bonds are more sensitive to interest rate changes.
2. **Credit Risk (Default Risk)**:
   - The risk that the bond issuer may be unable to make interest payments or repay the principal at maturity. This risk is higher for corporate bonds and lower for

government bonds.

3. **Inflation Risk**:
   - The risk that inflation will erode the purchasing power of the interest payments and the principal repayment.

4. **Liquidity Risk**:
   - The risk that an investor may not be able to buy or sell a bond easily without affecting its price. Less liquid bonds are harder to trade.

5. **Call Risk**:
   - The risk that a bond issuer may repay (call) the bond before its maturity date, usually when interest rates have fallen, leading to reinvestment risk for the bondholder.

Strategies for Investing in Bonds

1. **Laddering**:
   - Build a bond ladder by purchasing bonds with staggered maturities. This provides regular income and reduces interest rate risk as bonds mature at different times.

2. **Barbell Strategy**:
   - Invest in short-term and long-term bonds, but not intermediate-term bonds. This strategy aims to balance the higher yields of long-term bonds with the lower risk and greater liquidity of short-term bonds.

3. **Bond Funds and ETFs**:
   - Bond mutual funds and exchange-traded funds (ETFs) provide diversification and professional management. These funds invest in a portfolio of bonds, which can be more accessible for individual investors than purchasing individual bonds.

4. **Credit Analysis**:
   - Assess the creditworthiness of bond issuers using credit ratings from agencies like Moody's, Standard & Poor's, and Fitch. Higher-rated bonds are generally safer but offer lower yields.

Conclusion

Bonds and fixed-income investments play a critical role in a diversified investment portfolio. They provide a steady income stream and help mitigate risk, especially in volatile markets. Understanding the types of bonds, how they generate returns, and the associated risks will help you make informed decisions and build a balanced investment strategy. In the next chapter, we will explore mutual funds and ETFs, delving into their structures, benefits, and how to choose the right ones for your portfolio.

Chapter 8: Exploring Mutual Funds and ETFs

Introduction to Mutual Funds and ETFs

Mutual funds and exchange-traded funds (ETFs) are popular investment vehicles that pool money from multiple investors to purchase a diversified portfolio of assets. They offer several benefits, including professional management, diversification, and liquidity.

1. **What is a Mutual Fund?**
   - **Definition**: A mutual fund is an investment vehicle managed by professional portfolio managers who invest the fund's capital in a variety of assets, such as stocks, bonds, and other securities.
   - **Structure**: Investors buy shares in the mutual fund, and the value of these shares is based on the fund's net asset value (NAV), which is calculated at the end of each trading day.
   - **Types of Mutual Funds**:
     - **Equity Funds**: Invest primarily in stocks.
     - **Bond Funds**: Invest primarily in bonds.
     - **Balanced Funds**: Invest in a mix of stocks and bonds.
     - **Index Funds**: Aim to replicate the performance of a specific index, such as the S&P 500.
     - **Sector Funds**: Focus on specific sectors like technology, healthcare, or energy.
     - **Money Market Funds**: Invest in short-term, low-risk securities.

2. **What is an ETF?**
   - **Definition**: An ETF is similar to a mutual fund but trades on stock exchanges like individual stocks. ETFs aim to track the performance of a specific index, sector, commodity, or asset class.
   - **Structure**: ETFs offer intraday liquidity, meaning they can be bought and sold throughout the trading day at market prices.
   - **Types of ETFs**:
     - **Stock ETFs**: Track specific stock indices or sectors.
     - **Bond ETFs**: Track various types of bond indices.
     - **Commodity ETFs**: Track the price of

commodities like gold or oil.
- **International ETFs**: Track stock indices or sectors in specific countries or regions.
- **Thematic ETFs**: Focus on specific investment themes, such as technology, clean energy, or healthcare innovation.

Benefits of Mutual Funds and ETFs

1. **Diversification**:
   - Both mutual funds and ETFs provide instant diversification by pooling money from many investors to buy a variety of assets. This reduces the risk associated with investing in individual securities.
2. **Professional Management**:
   - Mutual funds are managed by professional portfolio managers who conduct research, select investments, and monitor the portfolio. Some ETFs are also actively managed, though many passively track an index.
3. **Liquidity**:
   - Mutual fund shares can be bought or sold at the fund's NAV at the end of the trading day. ETFs offer greater liquidity, as they can be traded on stock exchanges throughout the trading day.
4. **Cost Efficiency**:
   - ETFs often have lower expense ratios compared to mutual funds, particularly those that are passively managed. Index mutual funds also tend to have lower fees compared to actively managed funds.
5. **Accessibility**:
   - Both mutual funds and ETFs are accessible to individual investors, often with low minimum investment requirements.

How to Choose the Right Mutual Fund or ETF

1. **Investment Goals**:
   - Define your investment goals, such as retirement, buying a home, or funding education. This will help you choose funds that align with your objectives.
2. **Risk Tolerance**:
   - Assess your risk tolerance and choose funds that match your comfort level with risk. Equity funds and stock ETFs are generally riskier than bond funds and bond ETFs.
3. **Fund Performance**:
   - Review the historical performance of the mutual fund or

ETF. While past performance is not indicative of future results, it can provide insight into how the fund has performed in different market conditions.

4. **Expense Ratios**:
   - Compare the expense ratios of different funds. Lower expense ratios can significantly impact long-term returns, as high fees can erode gains over time.

5. **Fund Manager**:
   - For actively managed mutual funds, consider the experience and track record of the fund manager. A skilled manager can add value through active management.

6. **Index Tracking**:
   - For index funds and ETFs, check how closely the fund tracks its benchmark index. A low tracking error indicates the fund is effectively replicating the index's performance.

7. **Fund Holdings**:
   - Examine the fund's holdings to ensure they align with your investment strategy. This includes understanding the sectors, regions, and asset classes the fund invests in.

8. **Turnover Ratio**:
   - The turnover ratio indicates how frequently the fund buys and sells its holdings. High turnover can result in higher transaction costs and tax implications.

Tax Considerations

1. **Capital Gains**:
   - Mutual funds distribute capital gains to investors, which can result in tax liabilities. ETFs are generally more tax-efficient due to their structure, which minimizes capital gains distributions.

2. **Dividends**:
   - Both mutual funds and ETFs can generate dividend income, which may be subject to taxes. Qualified dividends are taxed at a lower rate compared to ordinary income.

3. **Tax-Advantaged Accounts**:
   - Consider holding mutual funds and ETFs in tax-advantaged accounts like IRAs or 401(k)s to defer or reduce taxes on investment gains.

Common Pitfalls to Avoid

1. **Chasing Performance**:
   - Avoid choosing funds solely based on recent high performance. High returns in the short term may not be

sustainable, and past performance does not guarantee future results.
2. **Overlooking Fees**:
   - Be mindful of the fees associated with mutual funds and ETFs. High expense ratios can significantly impact your investment returns over time.
3. **Ignoring Diversification**:
   - Even within mutual funds and ETFs, ensure you maintain a diversified portfolio. Avoid over-concentration in specific sectors or asset classes.
4. **Not Reviewing Investments Regularly**:
   - Regularly review your investments to ensure they continue to align with your goals and risk tolerance. Rebalance your portfolio as needed.

Conclusion

Mutual funds and ETFs offer investors a convenient way to achieve diversification, professional management, and potential for growth. By understanding the different types of funds, assessing your investment goals and risk tolerance, and being mindful of costs and tax implications, you can make informed decisions that enhance your investment strategy. In the next chapter, we will delve into the world of real estate investing, exploring various ways to invest in real estate and the benefits and risks associated with this asset class.

Chapter 9: The Essentials of Real Estate Investing

Introduction to Real Estate Investing

Real estate investing involves purchasing property as an investment to generate income rather than using it as a primary residence. It can provide significant returns through rental income, appreciation, and tax benefits. Here's an overview of the basics of real estate investing:
1. **Types of Real Estate Investments**:
   - **Residential Properties**: Single-family homes, multi-family homes, condos, and townhouses.
   - **Commercial Properties**: Office buildings, retail spaces, warehouses, and industrial properties.
   - **Vacation Properties**: Short-term rental properties in desirable vacation locations.
   - **Raw Land**: Undeveloped land purchased for future

development or resource extraction.

Benefits of Real Estate Investing

1. **Steady Income**:
   - Rental properties provide a regular income stream through monthly rent payments.
2. **Appreciation**:
   - Over time, real estate tends to appreciate in value. This appreciation can result in substantial capital gains when the property is sold.
3. **Tax Advantages**:
   - Real estate investors can take advantage of various tax deductions, such as mortgage interest, property taxes, operating expenses, depreciation, and repairs.
4. **Leverage**:
   - Investors can use borrowed capital (mortgages) to increase the potential return on investment. This is known as leveraging.
5. **Inflation Hedge**:
   - Real estate often acts as a hedge against inflation, as property values and rents typically rise with inflation.

Risks of Real Estate Investing

1. **Market Risk**:
   - Real estate markets can be volatile, and property values can decrease due to economic downturns, changes in the local market, or other factors.
2. **Liquidity Risk**:
   - Real estate is not as liquid as stocks or bonds. Selling a property can take time and may not always be possible at the desired price.
3. **Property Management**:
   - Managing rental properties can be time-consuming and may require dealing with maintenance issues, tenant disputes, and vacancies.
4. **Financing Risk**:
   - Changes in interest rates can impact mortgage payments. Additionally, obtaining financing for real estate investments can be challenging.
5. **Legal and Regulatory Risks**:
   - Real estate investments are subject to various local, state, and federal regulations, including zoning laws, tenant rights, and property taxes.

How to Invest in Real Estate

1. **Direct Property Ownership**:
   - **Buying Residential Rental Properties**:
     - Purchase a property to rent out to tenants. This provides rental income and potential appreciation.
   - **Investing in Commercial Properties**:
     - Purchase commercial properties to lease to businesses. This can provide higher rental income compared to residential properties but may also involve higher risks and management complexities.
   - **House Flipping**:
     - Buy properties at a lower price, renovate them, and sell them at a higher price. This strategy requires knowledge of the real estate market and construction.
2. **Real Estate Investment Trusts (REITs)**:
   - **Definition**: REITs are companies that own, operate, or finance income-producing real estate. They pool capital from multiple investors to purchase properties.
   - **Types**:
     - **Equity REITs**: Invest in and own properties. Revenue is generated through leasing space and collecting rents.
     - **Mortgage REITs (mREITs)**: Invest in and own property mortgages. Revenue is generated through the interest on the mortgage loans.
     - **Hybrid REITs**: Combine both equity and mortgage investments.
   - **Benefits**: REITs provide liquidity, diversification, and regular income through dividends. They are traded on major stock exchanges, making them accessible to individual investors.
3. **Real Estate Crowdfunding**:
   - **Definition**: Real estate crowdfunding platforms allow investors to pool their money to invest in real estate projects. These platforms typically offer both equity and debt investments.
   - **Benefits**: Lower capital requirements compared to direct ownership, access to a variety of projects, and potential for high returns.
   - **Risks**: These investments can be illiquid and may involve higher risk compared to REITs and direct ownership.

4. **Real Estate Partnerships**:
   - **Definition**: Real estate partnerships involve pooling resources with other investors to purchase and manage properties. These partnerships can take various forms, such as limited partnerships or joint ventures.
   - **Benefits**: Access to larger properties and projects, shared responsibilities, and combined expertise.
   - **Risks**: Partnership agreements can be complex, and disagreements among partners can arise.

Steps to Get Started in Real Estate Investing

1. **Set Clear Goals**:
   - Determine your investment objectives, such as generating rental income, achieving long-term appreciation, or diversifying your portfolio.
2. **Conduct Market Research**:
   - Study the local real estate market to understand trends, property values, rental rates, and demand. Identify areas with growth potential.
3. **Secure Financing**:
   - Explore different financing options, such as conventional mortgages, FHA loans, or private financing. Consider your credit score, down payment, and loan terms.
4. **Analyze Properties**:
   - Evaluate potential properties based on location, condition, price, and rental income potential. Use metrics like the cap rate (capitalization rate) and cash-on-cash return to assess profitability.
5. **Perform Due Diligence**:
   - Conduct thorough inspections and assessments of the property. Review property records, zoning laws, and any existing leases or tenant agreements.
6. **Develop a Management Plan**:
   - Decide whether you will manage the property yourself or hire a property management company. Consider the costs and responsibilities involved in property management.
7. **Close the Deal**:
   - Work with a real estate agent, attorney, and lender to finalize the purchase. Ensure all legal and financial aspects are in order before closing the deal.
8. **Monitor and Maintain the Property**:
   - Regularly monitor the property's condition, handle maintenance and repairs promptly, and maintain good

relationships with tenants.
Conclusion
Real estate investing offers numerous opportunities for generating income, achieving long-term growth, and diversifying your investment portfolio. By understanding the types of real estate investments, evaluating the benefits and risks, and following a strategic approach, you can make informed decisions and build a successful real estate investment portfolio. In the next chapter, we will delve into alternative investments, such as commodities, hedge funds, and cryptocurrencies, to further diversify your investment strategy.

Chapter 10: Exploring Alternative Investments

Introduction to Alternative Investments
Alternative investments encompass a wide range of non-traditional asset classes beyond stocks, bonds, and cash. These investments often have unique characteristics, including low correlation to traditional markets, potential for higher returns, and different risk profiles. Here's an overview of some common alternative investments:

1. **Commodities**:
   - Commodities are raw materials or agricultural products that can be bought and sold, such as gold, silver, oil, natural gas, corn, and coffee. Investing in commodities provides exposure to global supply and demand dynamics, inflation protection, and portfolio diversification.

2. **Hedge Funds**:
   - Hedge funds are investment funds that pool capital from accredited investors and employ a variety of strategies to generate returns. These strategies can include long/short equity, global macro, event-driven, and arbitrage. Hedge funds often aim to deliver positive returns regardless of market conditions and may use leverage and derivatives to enhance performance.

3. **Private Equity**:
   - Private equity involves investing in privately held companies that are not listed on public stock exchanges. Private equity firms raise capital from investors to acquire, restructure, or invest in businesses with the goal of improving operations and ultimately selling them for a profit. Private equity investments are typically illiquid and require a long-term investment horizon.

4. **Venture Capital**:
   - Venture capital focuses on investing in early-stage or startup companies with high growth potential. Venture capitalists provide funding to entrepreneurs in exchange for equity ownership in the company. Venture capital investments carry high risks but can offer substantial returns if successful.
5. **Real Assets**:
   - Real assets include physical assets such as real estate, infrastructure, and natural resources. Investing in real assets provides exposure to tangible assets that have intrinsic value and can serve as inflation hedges. Real assets often have low correlation with traditional financial markets.
6. **Cryptocurrencies**:
   - Cryptocurrencies are digital or virtual currencies that use cryptography for security and operate on decentralized networks based on blockchain technology. Bitcoin, Ethereum, and Litecoin are some of the most well-known cryptocurrencies. Investing in cryptocurrencies offers opportunities for high returns but also involves significant volatility and regulatory risks.

Benefits of Alternative Investments
1. **Diversification**:
   - Alternative investments have low correlation with traditional asset classes like stocks and bonds, making them effective tools for portfolio diversification. Adding alternative investments to a portfolio can help reduce overall risk and enhance risk-adjusted returns.
2. **Potential for Higher Returns**:
   - Alternative investments often offer the potential for higher returns compared to traditional investments. Strategies such as leverage, active management, and access to unique opportunities can contribute to enhanced performance.
3. **Inflation Hedge**:
   - Many alternative investments, such as commodities, real estate, and natural resources, serve as inflation hedges. These assets have intrinsic value and tend to appreciate in value during inflationary periods.
4. **Access to Unique Opportunities**:
   - Alternative investments provide access to investment opportunities that are not available in traditional markets.

This includes early-stage companies, distressed assets, and niche sectors that may offer high growth potential.

Risks of Alternative Investments

1. **Lack of Liquidity**:
   - Many alternative investments are illiquid and cannot be easily bought or sold on public exchanges. This lack of liquidity can make it challenging to access funds when needed and may require long holding periods.

2. **Complexity**:
   - Alternative investments often involve complex strategies, structures, and regulatory considerations. Investors may require specialized knowledge or rely on professional advisors to navigate these complexities effectively.

3. **Higher Fees**:
   - Alternative investments typically have higher fees compared to traditional investments, including management fees, performance fees, and carried interest. These fees can erode investment returns over time.

4. **Volatility**:
   - Alternative investments, such as hedge funds and cryptocurrencies, can exhibit high levels of volatility and price fluctuations. Investors must be prepared for periods of significant price swings and potential losses.

5. **Regulatory and Legal Risks**:
   - Alternative investments are subject to regulatory oversight and may be subject to specific legal and compliance requirements. Changes in regulations or legal issues can impact the value and viability of these investments.

How to Invest in Alternative Investments

1. **Educate Yourself**:
   - Before investing in alternative investments, take the time to educate yourself about the different asset classes, strategies, and risks involved. Consider reading books, attending seminars, and consulting with financial professionals.

2. **Assess Your Risk Tolerance**:
   - Alternative investments can be riskier and more volatile than traditional investments. Evaluate your risk tolerance and investment objectives to determine if alternative investments are suitable for your portfolio.

3. **Diversify Your Portfolio**:
   - Incorporate alternative investments into a diversified

portfolio to reduce overall risk and enhance returns. Consider the role that alternative investments play in your portfolio allocation and how they complement other asset classes.

4. **Consider Professional Management**:
   - Many alternative investments, such as hedge funds and private equity funds, require a high level of expertise and resources to manage effectively. Consider investing through professionally managed funds or working with experienced investment managers.

5. **Perform Due Diligence**:
   - Before investing in alternative investments, conduct thorough due diligence on the investment opportunity, fund manager, and underlying assets. Review historical performance, track record, and risk management practices.

6. **Understand Fees and Costs**:
   - Be aware of the fees and costs associated with alternative investments, including management fees, performance fees, and other expenses. Evaluate the impact of these fees on investment returns and factor them into your decision-making process.

Conclusion

Alternative investments offer unique opportunities for diversification, potential for higher returns, and exposure to non-traditional asset classes. However, they also come with increased complexity, liquidity constraints, and higher fees. By understanding the benefits and risks of alternative investments, conducting thorough due diligence, and incorporating them thoughtfully into a diversified portfolio, investors can capitalize on the opportunities these asset classes offer while managing associated risks effectively. In the next chapter, we will explore the importance of risk management in investment portfolios and strategies for mitigating risk across different asset classes.

Chapter 11: Risk Management in Investment Portfolios

Understanding Risk in Investments

Risk is an inherent aspect of investing and refers to the uncertainty of future returns. While all investments carry some level of risk, different asset classes and investment strategies entail varying degrees of risk. Here are some key concepts to understand about risk in investments:

1. **Types of Investment Risk**:
   - **Market Risk**: Arises from fluctuations in the overall

market, such as economic conditions, geopolitical events, and market sentiment.

- **Credit Risk**: The risk that a borrower will fail to meet their obligations, resulting in a loss of principal or interest for investors.
- **Interest Rate Risk**: The risk that changes in interest rates will impact the value of fixed-income investments, such as bonds.
- **Liquidity Risk**: The risk that an investment cannot be sold or converted to cash quickly without a significant loss of value.
- **Inflation Risk**: The risk that inflation will erode the purchasing power of investment returns over time.
- **Currency Risk**: The risk that changes in exchange rates will affect the value of investments denominated in foreign currencies.

2. **Risk Tolerance**:
- Risk tolerance refers to an investor's willingness and ability to tolerate fluctuations in the value of their investments. It is influenced by factors such as investment goals, time horizon, financial situation, and emotional temperament.

Importance of Risk Management

Effective risk management is essential for protecting investment capital, achieving long-term goals, and preserving financial security. Here's why risk management matters in investment portfolios:

1. **Preservation of Capital**:
- Managing risk helps protect investment capital from significant losses during periods of market downturns or economic crises. By minimizing downside risk, investors can preserve their wealth and avoid irreparable damage to their portfolios.

2. **Achievement of Objectives**:
- Proper risk management ensures that investment portfolios remain aligned with investors' objectives, whether they are focused on capital preservation, income generation, growth, or a combination of these goals. By managing risk effectively, investors can increase the likelihood of achieving their desired outcomes.

3. **Mitigation of Emotional Bias**:
- Emotions such as fear and greed can influence investment decisions and lead to irrational behavior, such as panic

selling during market downturns or chasing speculative investments during bull markets. Risk management strategies help mitigate emotional bias by providing a disciplined framework for decision-making.

4. **Enhanced Long-Term Returns**:
   - By systematically managing risk, investors can optimize the risk-return trade-off in their portfolios. While riskier investments may offer higher potential returns, they also carry greater downside risk. A balanced approach to risk management allows investors to capture upside potential while mitigating the impact of adverse events.

Strategies for Risk Management
1. **Asset Allocation**:
   - Asset allocation involves spreading investment capital across different asset classes, such as stocks, bonds, cash, and alternative investments. Diversification helps reduce the impact of volatility in any single asset class and can enhance risk-adjusted returns.

2. **Diversification**:
   - Diversification within asset classes further reduces risk by investing in a variety of securities or instruments within each asset class. For example, within the stock market, investors can diversify across different industries, sectors, and geographic regions.

3. **Portfolio Rebalancing**:
   - Regular portfolio rebalancing involves periodically adjusting asset allocations to maintain desired risk levels and investment objectives. Rebalancing ensures that portfolios remain aligned with investors' risk tolerance and long-term goals.

4. **Use of Risk Management Tools**:
   - Investors can utilize various risk management tools and techniques to mitigate specific risks in their portfolios. For example, options and futures contracts can be used to hedge against market volatility and downside risk. Stop-loss orders can limit potential losses on individual investments.

5. **Stress Testing**:
   - Stress testing involves analyzing how investment portfolios perform under adverse scenarios, such as market downturns or economic recessions. By stress testing portfolios, investors can identify potential vulnerabilities

and make proactive adjustments to mitigate risk.

6. **Continuous Monitoring and Review**:
    - Risk management is an ongoing process that requires continuous monitoring and review of investment portfolios. Regularly assessing portfolio performance, market conditions, and changes in investors' circumstances allows for timely adjustments to risk management strategies.

Conclusion

Risk management is a critical component of successful investing, allowing investors to protect capital, achieve long-term objectives, and navigate uncertain market conditions. By understanding the types of investment risk, assessing risk tolerance, and implementing effective risk management strategies such as asset allocation, diversification, and portfolio rebalancing, investors can build resilient portfolios that withstand market volatility and generate consistent returns over time. In the next chapter, we will explore the importance of financial planning and how to develop a comprehensive financial plan to achieve your financial goals.

Chapter 12: The Importance of Financial Planning

Understanding Financial Planning

Financial planning is the process of setting and achieving financial goals through the effective management of finances, investments, and assets. It involves assessing your current financial situation, defining your goals, and developing a comprehensive strategy to achieve those goals. Here's why financial planning is essential for financial well-being:

1. **Goal Setting**:
    - Financial planning helps you identify and prioritize your financial goals, whether they include buying a home, saving for retirement, funding education, or starting a business. By setting clear objectives, you can create a roadmap for your financial future.

2. **Budgeting and Saving**:
    - Financial planning involves creating a budget to track income and expenses and allocating funds towards savings and investments. A well-defined budget helps you live within your means, build an emergency fund, and achieve your savings goals.

3. **Debt Management**:
    - Effective financial planning includes strategies for

managing and reducing debt, such as credit card debt, student loans, and mortgages. By prioritizing debt repayment and exploring debt consolidation options, you can minimize interest costs and improve your financial health.

4. **Investment Strategy**:
   - Financial planning guides investment decisions by aligning your investment strategy with your financial goals, risk tolerance, and time horizon. Whether you're investing in stocks, bonds, real estate, or alternative assets, a well-thought-out investment plan maximizes returns while minimizing risk.

5. **Retirement Planning**:
   - Planning for retirement is a crucial aspect of financial planning. It involves estimating retirement expenses, determining retirement income sources (such as pensions, Social Security, and investments), and developing a savings strategy to ensure a comfortable retirement lifestyle.

6. **Risk Management**:
   - Financial planning includes assessing and managing various financial risks, such as market risk, inflation risk, longevity risk, and health care costs. Insurance products, emergency funds, and estate planning are essential components of risk management.

Components of a Financial Plan

1. **Financial Goals**:
   - Identify short-term, medium-term, and long-term financial goals, such as buying a home, saving for education, retiring comfortably, or leaving a legacy for future generations.

2. **Net Worth Statement**:
   - Calculate your net worth by subtracting your liabilities (debts) from your assets (savings, investments, real estate, etc.). Your net worth provides a snapshot of your overall financial health.

3. **Cash Flow Analysis**:
   - Analyze your cash flow by tracking income and expenses over a specified period. Understanding your cash flow helps identify areas where you can reduce expenses and increase savings.

4. **Budgeting**:

- Develop a budget that outlines your income, fixed expenses (such as rent/mortgage, utilities, and insurance), variable expenses (such as groceries, entertainment, and dining out), and savings goals.

5. **Debt Management Plan**:
   - Create a strategy for paying off existing debts, prioritizing high-interest debts first. Consider debt consolidation or refinancing options to lower interest rates and streamline debt repayment.

6. **Investment Strategy**:
   - Define your investment objectives, risk tolerance, and time horizon. Develop an investment portfolio that aligns with your goals, diversifies risk, and maximizes returns while minimizing costs.

7. **Retirement Planning**:
   - Estimate your retirement expenses, determine your retirement income sources, and calculate how much you need to save to achieve your retirement goals. Consider tax-advantaged retirement accounts, such as 401(k)s and IRAs, and explore retirement income strategies.

8. **Insurance Coverage**:
   - Review your insurance needs, including health insurance, life insurance, disability insurance, and long-term care insurance. Ensure adequate coverage to protect against unexpected events and liabilities.

9. **Estate Planning**:
   - Develop an estate plan that outlines how your assets will be distributed upon your death and ensures your wishes are carried out. This may include drafting a will, establishing trusts, and designating beneficiaries for retirement accounts and life insurance policies.

Benefits of Financial Planning

1. **Clarity and Direction**:
   - Financial planning provides clarity and direction by helping you define your financial goals, prioritize your objectives, and develop actionable strategies to achieve them.

2. **Financial Security**:
   - A well-executed financial plan enhances financial security by establishing emergency funds, managing debt, protecting against risks, and building wealth over time.

3. **Peace of Mind**:

- Knowing that you have a comprehensive financial plan in place gives you peace of mind and reduces stress about money matters. You can approach financial decisions with confidence and adapt to changes in your circumstances.

4. **Optimized Resource Allocation**:
   - Financial planning optimizes resource allocation by ensuring that your income is used efficiently to support your goals and lifestyle while minimizing unnecessary expenses and waste.

5. **Adaptability and Flexibility**:
   - A financial plan is not static but evolves with changes in your life circumstances, financial goals, and market conditions. It provides a framework for adapting to new challenges and opportunities as they arise.

Conclusion

Financial planning is a fundamental aspect of personal finance that empowers individuals and families to achieve their financial goals, build wealth, and secure their financial futures. By taking a proactive approach to financial planning, you can gain clarity and direction, optimize resource allocation, and enjoy peace of mind knowing that you're on the path to financial success. In the next chapter, we will explore the role of behavioral psychology in investment decision-making and how understanding human behavior can influence investment outcomes.

Chapter 13: Behavioral Psychology in Investment Decision-Making

Understanding Behavioral Psychology

Behavioral psychology examines how human emotions, biases, and cognitive errors influence decision-making and behavior. In the context of investing, understanding behavioral psychology is essential for recognizing and mitigating common biases that can lead to irrational investment decisions. Here's an overview of key principles of behavioral psychology in investment decision-making:

1. **Emotional Bias**:
   - Emotions such as fear, greed, and overconfidence often drive investment decisions and can lead to irrational behavior. Fear of missing out (FOMO) may cause investors to chase hot investment trends, while fear of loss may prompt selling during market downturns.

2. **Herd Mentality**:

- Humans have a tendency to follow the crowd, especially in uncertain or volatile markets. This herd mentality can result in asset bubbles, market inefficiencies, and exaggerated price movements.

3. **Loss Aversion**:
    - Loss aversion refers to the tendency of investors to prefer avoiding losses over acquiring equivalent gains. Investors may hold onto losing investments longer than they should, hoping to avoid realizing a loss, even when it's against their best interests.

4. **Overconfidence**:
    - Overconfidence bias leads investors to overestimate their knowledge, skills, and ability to predict market movements. This can result in excessive trading, poor risk management, and underestimation of investment risks.

5. **Anchoring**:
    - Anchoring bias occurs when investors rely too heavily on a specific piece of information or reference point when making decisions. For example, investors may anchor their expectations for future stock prices based on past performance or analyst price targets.

6. **Confirmation Bias**:
    - Confirmation bias causes investors to seek out information that confirms their existing beliefs or opinions while ignoring or discounting contradictory evidence. This can lead to selective attention and overconfidence in investment decisions.

Impact of Behavioral Biases on Investment Outcomes
1. **Suboptimal Decision-Making**:
    - Behavioral biases can lead to suboptimal investment decisions that deviate from rational, evidence-based strategies. This can result in missed opportunities, excessive risk-taking, and diminished investment returns over time.

2. **Market Volatility**:
    - Behavioral biases contribute to market volatility by amplifying investor sentiment and exacerbating price fluctuations. Herd behavior, panic selling, and irrational exuberance can lead to market bubbles and crashes.

3. **Underperformance**:
    - Investors who succumb to behavioral biases often underperform the broader market or benchmark indices.

Emotional decision-making, frequent trading, and failure to adhere to an investment plan can erode investment returns and hinder long-term wealth accumulation.

4. **Loss of Capital**:
   - Behavioral biases can lead to significant losses of capital, especially during periods of market turbulence or economic downturns. Emotional responses to market fluctuations may cause investors to panic sell at low prices, locking in losses rather than staying the course and riding out market cycles.

Strategies for Mitigating Behavioral Biases

1. **Awareness and Education**:
   - Awareness of common behavioral biases is the first step toward mitigating their impact on investment decisions. Educate yourself about behavioral psychology principles and recognize when biases may be influencing your thinking.

2. **Emotional Discipline**:
   - Practice emotional discipline by staying calm and rational during periods of market volatility. Avoid making impulsive decisions based on fear, greed, or overconfidence. Stick to your investment plan and long-term goals.

3. **Diversification**:
   - Diversification helps mitigate the impact of individual investment decisions by spreading risk across different asset classes, industries, and geographic regions. A well-diversified portfolio can reduce the impact of specific investment failures or market downturns.

4. **Adherence to Investment Plan**:
   - Develop and adhere to a clearly defined investment plan that aligns with your financial goals, risk tolerance, and time horizon. Regularly review and rebalance your portfolio as needed, but avoid making knee-jerk reactions to short-term market fluctuations.

5. **Seeking Objective Advice**:
   - Consider seeking advice from a qualified financial advisor who can provide objective, evidence-based guidance and help you avoid common behavioral pitfalls. An experienced advisor can offer perspective, discipline, and accountability in the investment decision-making process.

6. **Continuous Learning and Improvement**:

- Stay informed about market trends, investment strategies, and behavioral psychology research. Continuously evaluate your own investment decisions and learn from both successes and failures to improve your decision-making process over time.

Conclusion

Behavioral psychology plays a significant role in investment decision-making, influencing emotions, biases, and cognitive errors that can lead to irrational behavior and suboptimal outcomes. By understanding common behavioral biases, recognizing their impact on investment decisions, and implementing strategies to mitigate their effects, investors can make more informed, disciplined, and successful investment decisions. In the next chapter, we will explore the role of technology in finance and how technological advancements are transforming the way we manage money, invest, and access financial services.

Chapter 14: The Role of Technology in Finance

Introduction to FinTech

Financial technology, often referred to as FinTech, encompasses the use of technology to improve and automate financial services, processes, and products. From online banking and mobile payments to robo-advisors and blockchain technology, FinTech innovations are reshaping the financial industry and transforming the way we manage money, invest, and access financial services. Here's an overview of the role of technology in finance:

1. **Digital Banking**:
   - Digital banking platforms allow customers to access banking services and manage their finances online or through mobile apps. These platforms offer features such as account management, bill payments, fund transfers, and remote deposit capture, providing convenience and accessibility to users.
2. **Mobile Payments**:
   - Mobile payment solutions enable users to make transactions using their smartphones or other mobile devices. Whether it's peer-to-peer payments, in-store purchases, or online shopping, mobile payment apps like Apple Pay, Google Pay, and PayPal offer secure, fast, and convenient payment options.
3. **Robo-Advisors**:
   - Robo-advisors are automated investment platforms that

use algorithms and artificial intelligence to provide investment advice and manage portfolios. These platforms offer low-cost, diversified investment options tailored to investors' goals, risk tolerance, and time horizon, democratizing access to investment management services.

4. **Blockchain and Cryptocurrencies**:
   - Blockchain technology, the underlying technology behind cryptocurrencies like Bitcoin and Ethereum, enables secure, decentralized transactions and digital asset ownership. Cryptocurrencies offer alternative forms of currency and investment opportunities, while blockchain has potential applications in areas such as supply chain management, voting systems, and identity verification.

5. **Peer-to-Peer Lending**:
   - Peer-to-peer lending platforms connect borrowers directly with individual or institutional investors, bypassing traditional financial institutions. These platforms facilitate borrowing and lending activities, offering competitive interest rates and streamlined loan approval processes.

6. **Artificial Intelligence and Big Data**:
   - Artificial intelligence and big data analytics are used in various financial applications, including fraud detection, credit scoring, risk assessment, and investment analysis. Machine learning algorithms analyze vast amounts of data to uncover patterns, trends, and insights that inform decision-making and improve financial outcomes.

Benefits of FinTech

1. **Convenience and Accessibility**:
   - FinTech solutions offer convenience and accessibility, allowing users to access financial services anytime, anywhere, using digital devices. Whether it's checking account balances, transferring funds, or managing investments, users can perform tasks quickly and efficiently.

2. **Cost-Effectiveness**:
   - FinTech innovations often come with lower costs compared to traditional financial services. Digital banking reduces overhead costs associated with physical branches, while robo-advisors offer investment management services at a fraction of the cost of traditional financial advisors.

3. **Financial Inclusion**:
   - FinTech has the potential to promote financial inclusion by

providing access to financial services for underserved populations, including the unbanked and underbanked. Mobile banking, digital payments, and microfinance platforms expand access to banking and credit services, empowering individuals and communities to participate in the formal financial system.

4. **Innovation and Customization**:
   - FinTech fosters innovation and customization in financial services, with startups and established companies alike introducing new products and services to meet evolving consumer needs. From personalized investment portfolios to tailored insurance products, FinTech solutions offer flexibility and choice for consumers.

5. **Transparency and Security**:
   - FinTech platforms prioritize transparency and security, leveraging technologies such as encryption, biometrics, and distributed ledgers to safeguard user data and financial transactions. Blockchain technology, in particular, enhances transparency and immutability in financial transactions, reducing the risk of fraud and manipulation.

Challenges and Considerations

1. **Regulatory Compliance**:
   - FinTech companies must navigate complex regulatory landscapes and comply with regulatory requirements governing financial services. Regulatory uncertainty and compliance costs can pose challenges for startups and incumbents alike.

2. **Cybersecurity Risks**:
   - As FinTech solutions rely on digital technologies, they are susceptible to cybersecurity threats such as data breaches, phishing attacks, and malware infections. Ensuring robust cybersecurity measures and data protection protocols is critical to maintaining trust and security in FinTech platforms.

3. **Privacy Concerns**:
   - The collection and use of personal data by FinTech companies raise privacy concerns among consumers and regulators. Balancing the benefits of data-driven innovation with privacy rights and data protection regulations is an ongoing challenge for the FinTech industry.

4. **Digital Divide**:

- While FinTech offers opportunities for financial inclusion, disparities in access to technology and digital literacy can widen the digital divide. Ensuring equitable access to FinTech solutions and addressing barriers to adoption among marginalized communities is essential for promoting financial inclusion and reducing socioeconomic inequalities.

Future Trends in FinTech

1. **Continued Innovation**:
   - FinTech innovation is expected to accelerate, with advancements in artificial intelligence, blockchain, biometrics, and quantum computing driving new applications and business models in financial services.
2. **Collaboration and Partnerships**:
   - Collaboration between FinTech startups, established financial institutions, and regulatory authorities will foster innovation, improve interoperability, and address regulatory challenges in the FinTech ecosystem.
3. **Focus on Sustainability**:
   - FinTech solutions are increasingly focusing on sustainability and responsible investing, with initiatives to promote environmental, social, and governance (ESG) criteria in investment decisions and financial products.
4. **Global Expansion**:
   - FinTech adoption is expanding globally, with emerging markets embracing digital financial services to address financial inclusion challenges and drive economic growth. Cross-border partnerships and regulatory harmonization efforts will facilitate FinTech expansion across regions.

Conclusion

FinTech is revolutionizing the financial industry, offering innovative solutions that enhance convenience, accessibility, and efficiency in financial services. From digital banking and mobile payments to blockchain and artificial intelligence, FinTech innovations are transforming how individuals and businesses manage money, invest, and access financial services. While FinTech presents opportunities for financial inclusion, cost-effectiveness, and innovation, it also poses challenges related to regulation, cybersecurity, and privacy. By embracing technological advancements, fostering collaboration, and addressing key challenges, the FinTech industry can drive positive change and shape the future of finance on a global scale. In the next chapter, we will explore the concept of financial literacy and its importance in empowering individuals to make informed financial decisions.

Chapter 15: The Importance of Financial Literacy

Understanding Financial Literacy

Financial literacy refers to the knowledge, skills, and understanding of financial concepts and principles that enable individuals to make informed and effective financial decisions. From managing personal finances and budgeting to investing, saving for retirement, and understanding financial products and services, financial literacy plays a crucial role in empowering individuals to achieve their financial goals and build long-term financial security. Here's why financial literacy is essential:

1. **Personal Finance Management**:
   - Financial literacy equips individuals with the knowledge and skills to manage their personal finances effectively. This includes creating and sticking to a budget, tracking expenses, managing debt, and saving for short-term and long-term goals.
2. **Investment Decision-Making**:
   - Understanding financial concepts such as risk, return, diversification, and asset allocation is essential for making informed investment decisions. Financially literate individuals can evaluate investment options, assess risk-reward trade-offs, and build investment portfolios that align with their goals and risk tolerance.
3. **Retirement Planning**:
   - Financial literacy is crucial for retirement planning, helping individuals estimate their retirement needs, identify retirement income sources, such as pensions, Social Security, and savings, and develop strategies to achieve a comfortable retirement lifestyle.
4. **Consumer Protection**:
   - Financially literate consumers are better equipped to navigate the complex landscape of financial products and services, understand terms and conditions, compare offers, and avoid predatory practices and scams. Financial literacy empowers individuals to make sound financial decisions and protect themselves from exploitation.

5. **Economic Stability**:
   - A financially literate population contributes to economic stability and prosperity by promoting responsible financial behavior, reducing financial stress and vulnerability, and fostering a culture of saving, investing, and wealth accumulation.

Challenges and Barriers to Financial Literacy

1. **Lack of Education**:
   - Many individuals lack access to formal financial education and resources, leading to gaps in financial knowledge and skills. Limited education on personal finance topics in schools and communities contributes to low levels of financial literacy among the general population.

2. **Complexity of Financial Products**:
   - Financial products and services can be complex and difficult to understand, especially for individuals with limited financial literacy. Complex terminology, fees, and fine print can deter consumers from engaging with financial products and make it challenging to make informed decisions.

3. **Behavioral Biases**:
   - Behavioral biases, such as overconfidence, inertia, and present bias, can hinder financial decision-making and undermine efforts to improve financial literacy. Individuals may procrastinate financial planning, rely on faulty heuristics, or succumb to emotional impulses that lead to suboptimal outcomes.

4. **Cultural and Socioeconomic Factors**:
   - Cultural norms, socioeconomic status, and access to resources can influence levels of financial literacy within communities. Disparities in education, income, and access to financial services contribute to inequalities in financial literacy and exacerbate socioeconomic inequalities.

Strategies for Promoting Financial Literacy

1. **Early Education**:
   - Integrate financial education into school curricula at an early age to build foundational knowledge and skills in personal finance, budgeting, saving, and investing. Empower young people to develop healthy financial habits and make informed financial decisions as they transition into adulthood.

2. **Accessible Resources**:

- Provide accessible and user-friendly resources, tools, and educational materials on personal finance topics to empower individuals to learn at their own pace. Utilize digital platforms, mobile apps, online courses, and community workshops to reach diverse audiences and address different learning styles.

3. **Community Engagement**:
   - Engage with communities and grassroots organizations to promote financial literacy initiatives tailored to local needs and priorities. Collaborate with schools, libraries, nonprofits, and employers to deliver financial education programs and resources to underserved populations.

4. **Public Awareness Campaigns**:
   - Launch public awareness campaigns to raise awareness of the importance of financial literacy and encourage individuals to take proactive steps to improve their financial knowledge and skills. Leverage media, social networks, and public events to promote financial literacy initiatives and resources.

5. **Institutional Support**:
   - Financial institutions, employers, and government agencies play a vital role in promoting financial literacy through employee training programs, consumer education initiatives, and policy advocacy. Support institutional efforts to integrate financial literacy into organizational practices and policies.

Conclusion

Financial literacy is a fundamental skill that empowers individuals to make informed financial decisions, achieve their goals, and build long-term financial security. By understanding key financial concepts, practicing responsible financial habits, and accessing resources and support, individuals can enhance their financial literacy and improve their financial well-being. Promoting financial literacy requires a multifaceted approach that involves education, outreach, community engagement, and institutional support. By investing in financial education and empowering individuals to take control of their finances, we can create a more financially resilient and prosperous society for all.